Enid Blyton's

· BIBLE · STORIES ·

THE BABY IN THE BULRUSHES

& THE KIND PRINCESS

OLD TESTAMENT
BOOK 6

GRANADA PUBLISHING

2

THE BABY IN THE BULRUSHES

The brothers of Joseph, the chief man of Egypt, were very happy in their new land. Pharaoh was kind to them, and they became rich and powerful.

They were quite different from the Egyptians around them. They had different ways, and they prayed to a different God. As long as Joseph was alive, and Pharaoh was good to them, things went well with the Children of Jacob.

But after Joseph was dead, and his Pharaoh was dead too, there came a new King, a Pharaoh who did not like the Children of Jacob – or Children of Israel, as they were now called.

Pharaoh saw that these strangers were becoming very rich and very powerful. He spoke to his chief men about them.

"What shall we do with these men, the Children of Israel?" he said. "See how mighty they are! They overrun our land, and maybe when we go to war, these men will join our enemies, and fight us."

"What are your commands, lord?" asked the chief men.

4

"We will set masters over them," said Pharaoh. "We will make them into slaves. We will order them to work for us. They shall build me treasure-houses, they shall make roads and dig canals."

So masters were put over the Children of Israel, and they were used as slaves, and made to work very hard.

They worked out in the hot sun, with little food to eat, and no wages. They made bricks from the river clay. They put chopped straw with the clay to bind it together, and then the hot sun baked the bricks.

The Egyptian masters beat them cruelly, forcing them to work harder and harder. But still it seemed as if the Children of Israel became greater in numbers, and were to be found over all the land.

Pharaoh saw the great number of the

Israelites, the Children of Israel, and he gave a terrible command.

"Take every boy-baby from its mother, and throw it into the river Nile," he said. "Then there will be no more young Israelite men growing up."

The women were full of woe when they heard this. They wept bitterly when their little baby boys were taken away and thrown into the river.

There was one mother called Jochabed. She had a beautiful baby son, healthy and strong, and she was afraid that the Egyptians would come and take him away from her. She had another boy Aaron, and a little daughter Miriam. They were safe – but how could she save her baby boy?

"I will hide him," said Jochabed. "The Egyptians shall not take him." So she hid him in her house, but as he grew he cried very

loudly, and the mother was afraid that a passing
Egyptian might hear him.

So Jochabed thought of a plan. She called
her daughter Miriam to her and told her.

"We will make a little ark out of the bulrushes,"
she said. "It shall be quite water-tight, and I
will put a soft lining to it. Then we will put the

little ark among the reeds, near to the place where the Egyptian princess comes to bathe herself each morning."

Miriam was sent to get the rushes. She knew quite well how to make a basket from them. Often the country women crossed the river by swimming, and in front of them they would

sometimes push their baby, safe in a basket of bulrushes.

Miriam and her mother set to work to make the little ark. "It must be just the right size for our baby," said his mother. "We will weave a lid for the ark too, so that the sun will not beat down on his dear little face."

They made a strong little basket, the right size for the growing baby. It had a lid that could be opened and shut.

"Now we will daub it with slime and pitch," said Jochabed. "Then no water will get through the cracks and sink the little ark."

They daubed it well and set it out in the hot sun to dry. When it was quite dry and water-tight, they took it into the house to line it with soft blankets. It looked a dear little ark when they had finished.

"Now we will put our baby in it," said

Jochabed, and she lifted the child and laid him gently into the ark. He lay there on the little rugs, smiling up at them. His mother wept to see him. It was so hard to part from such a lovely child.

When he was asleep Jochabed told Miriam it was time to take him down to the river. So, carrying the ark between them, they slipped down to the water, waiting until there was no one to see them.

"Here are some reeds," said Miriam. "Let us put him there. He will be well hidden."

They went to the reeds that waved and whispered in the wind. They set the ark on the waters, and it floated beautifully.

Jochabed lifted up the lid and took a last look at the sleeping child. "Goodbye, my little one," she said, and the tears streamed down her face.

She turned to go, and then spoke to Miriam.
"Miriam, stay here and watch him," she said.
"Hide yourself away somewhere, in sight of
the ark. Watch to see what happens to our
poor little baby."

So, whilst Jochabed went home, weeping,
Miriam, hid herself, and watched the little
floating ark. What would happen to their
precious baby?

THE KIND PRINCESS

T he baby slept peacefully. He did not wake and he did not cry. Miriam stayed hidden, wondering if anyone would come.

At last she heard voices, and she peeped from her hiding-place and saw the beautiful Princess of Egypt coming down to bathe in the river. Her maids were with her, and they were all talking and laughing together.

"Go, walk by the river," said the Princess to her maids. "I need only one of you to help me to undress."

The Princess began to take off her clothes, looking at the cool water. She saw the reeds waving in the wind – and then her quick eye caught sight of something queer in the reeds.

"What is that?" she wondered. "It looks like a little boat made of rushes. What is inside?"

"Shall I go and see?" said her maid.

"Fetch it for me," said the Princess. "I would like to open it and see what there is in it. It is strange to see a little basket floating on the water."

The maid ran to the water. She lifted up the basket, which was heavy. She took it to the Princess.

The Princess lifted the lid of the basket —
and saw the beautiful, sleeping child inside.
He awoke, gazed up in fright, and began to
cry. His face puckered up, and tears streamed
down his rosy cheeks.

"What a lovely baby!" said the Princess, her
kind heart filled with pity. "Come here, little
one, let me hold you. Don't cry any more."

She lifted the baby from his little boat and
rocked him gently against her breast. She
looked at his dark, curly hair and his big
dark eyes.

He heard her kind voice and stopped crying.
Then he smiled, and the Princess lost her
heart to him.

"This must be one of the babies who were
meant to be thrown into the river Nile," said
the Princess, who knew all about the King's
command. "It is a child of one of the slaves. I

wish he were mine. He is so beautiful."

She cradled him in her arms, loving him. He felt warm and cuddlesome. She could not bear to think he might be thrown into the river and drowned.

Miriam was still watching from her hiding-place. She saw all that happened. She had held her breath when the maid fetched the little ark. Then how glad she was to see the Princess take up the baby and nurse him so lovingly!

"She loves our baby," thought Miriam in joy. "She is kind. Perhaps she will keep him. He is so lovely."

The little girl crept out of her hiding-place. She stood looking shyly at the Princess. The Princess saw her and smiled.

"Do you want a nurse for the baby?" said Miriam, anxiously. "He is small and he needs a nurse. Shall I fetch one of the slaves for

you? I know one who could nurse the child."

The Princess looked down at the baby and made up her mind to keep him. "Go," she said to Miriam. "Bring me someone to nurse this child and love him."

Miriam ran away without another word. She went to her home, and rushed to her mother.

Jochabed looked up, her face still stained with tears. "What is it?" she said. "What news have you of our baby?"

"Good news, mother!" said Miriam, joyfully. "The Princess came down to bathe and she found our little baby. She took him from the ark we made, and she nursed him in her arms

and loved him! She said she wished he were her own."

"Will he be safe then?" said Jochabed, in joy.

"Yes, he will," said Miriam, "and oh, mother, the Princess wants a nurse for him. You must come."

Jochabed hurried to the waterside with Miriam. She saw the great Princess there, the baby still in her arms. The Princess loved him, there was no doubt about that.

Jochabed stood near, and spoke humbly. "You want a nurse for the child, great Princess?"

The Princess looked up and smiled. "Yes," she said. "I have found this beautiful baby floating in an ark on the water among the bulrushes. I want a nurse for him, because when he is old enough I shall make him my own son. Will you take him and look after him for me until he grows into a fine boy?"

Jochabed could hardly speak for joy. She held out her arms for the baby. The Princess put him into them and the child crowed and smiled. He knew his mother.

Then the Princess guessed that Jochabed was really his mother, and she knew that he would be well cared for and loved. "Look after him well," she said. "I will pay you wages, and, when the time comes, you shall bring him to me, and he shall live with me, and be like a little prince."

Jochabed took her baby away, rejoicing. Miriam went with her, very happy too. Now their baby would not be taken away and drowned, he would belong to them, and grow up with them.

"One day, my little one, you must leave me, and go to the palace," said Jochabed, as she

bathed him that night. "But that day is far off. Till then you belong to me, and I shall love you, and you shall love me."

"You will not need to hide him any more, Mother," said Miriam. "The Princess will not allow the soldiers to harm him. We can take him with us wherever we go."

So no longer was the baby hidden away, but lived happily with his family, growing stronger and bigger every month.

The Princess did not forget the baby she had taken from the waters. She thought of him often, and made plans for the day when the

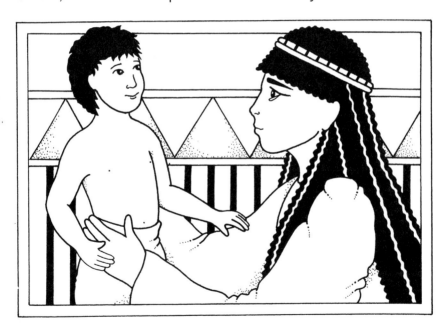

child should come to the palace and be her own little son.

He shall learn many things," she said. "He shall have fine clothes, and he shall have servants of his own. I shall love him dearly."

The baby grew well. He talked and he walked. Soon he was old enough to leave his mother and go to the Princess.

One day his mother took him to the palace. She said goodbye to him, for now he must dress as an Egyptian, and learn the ways of the over-lords, and forget that he was the son of a slave.

The Princess was proud of the beautiful boy. She drew him to her lovingly.

"I shall call you 'Moses'," she said. "That means 'Taken from the waters', little son."

And so the boy was known as Moses, the child taken from the waters. He was brought up as a prince, and wore fine clothes and ate good food. He was taught many things and grew up into a strong and wise youth.

But he never forgot that he was the son of a slave, and he pitied his people as he saw them toiling day by day in the hot sun.

"One day," he thought, "I will rescue them. I will be their leader, and they shall follow me."

·THE·END·